After the Dust Settles

After the Dust Settles

Dr. Cassundra White-Elliott

This book is a work of non-fiction. Some names have been changed to protect people's identities and their privacy; however, all details are true according to the author's perspective.

Published by CLF Publishing, LLC. 3281 Guasti Road, Seventh Floor, Ontario, CA 91761. (760) 669-8149.

Copyright © 2013 by Cassundra White-Elliott. All rights reserved. No portion of this book may be reproduced, stored in a retrieval system, or transmitted by any form or any means electronically, photocopied, recorded, or any other except for brief quotations in printed reviews, without the prior permission of the publisher.

Cover Design by Senir Design. Contact information- info@senirdesign.com.

ISBN # **978-0-9884237-8-7**

Printed in the United States of America.

Dedications

I dedicate this book to all persons who inspired each chapter. Without them, there would have not been any instances for 'the dust to settle' and for me to need an emotional healing.

Table of Contents

Prologue	9
Introduction	11
The Loss of a Matriarch	17
A Moment of Reflection- Dealing with Death	36
The Friend who Became a Client	39
A Moment of Reflection- Doing Business	63
Under Duress	67
A Moment of Reflection- Serving the Lord	80
A Mother's Heartbreak	83
A Moment of Reflection- Relationship Woes	94
Oh, Lord! Hear my Cry!	97
A Moment of Reflection- Living a Spirit-Filled Life	106
The Gift of Salvation	109
About the Author	115
Other Books by the Author	117

Prologue

In 2005, I wrote my best seller *Unleashed Anger, Anger Unleashed.* This book shares my testimonial of being healed and delivered from uncontrollable anger. The writing of the book took nine months, which according to my 'normal' writing pattern was not normal. However, everything is done in God's timing. The writing of the book, in the nine-month time span, was necessary for my healing and deliverance from unhealthy anger-driven behaviors.

Prior to writing *Unleashed Anger, Unleashed Anger*, I was ordained by God to write my autobiography. When I attempted to write my autobiography as I was instructed, I began to have flashbacks of my past. These flashbacks made it virtually impossible to write my life's story because I began to remember horrible incidents which occurred during my childhood. As a result, the book that would minister healing to me was birthed: *Unleashed Anger, Anger Unleashed*.

In 2007, I wrote another book that ministered healing and deliverance to me titled *Through the Storm*. However, it would not be for another two years that I would write my autobiography. In 2009, after my fortieth birthday and upon completion of my doctoral degree, *From Despair, through Determination, to Victory!* (my autobiography) was written and published.

Three and a half years later, after the writing of my autobiography and after several requests to tell more of my story, this book *After the Dust Settles* was birthed. As life carried on, my saga continued. As with anyone else, my life had its share of ups and downs. I am glad to say that the joys have been numerous, the pains have been few, and my anger has been released.

However, the pains and disappointments I experienced took my life in a different direction, with a different mindset: a mindset of being isolated, a mindset of being on guard with some while being free with others. Life comes as a lesson to teach, and I am determined to learn.

And so, here is my story, not in its entirety, but in a synoptic version of episodes.

As you read, may the Lord bless you to be ministered to. Maybe you have experienced similar situations and need a break through. This is the season for your release. Let God be the awesome, powerful and holy God that He is who can set captives free. In the name of the Lord Jesus, be free today!

Introduction

Life, although full of adventure, fascination, and wonderment, can also be filled with bewilderment, stress, disappointments and strife. Engaging in the joyful moments of life is a breeze. There is no stress involved at all. Contrary to enjoying life's joys is dealing with the not-so-pleasant moments life issues to each of us.

To keep a healthy balance, one must have a strategy for overcoming and dealing with life's troubles. Some prefer therapy sessions with a psychiatrist, while others prefer a night out with the guys or girls, so they can vent and/or get advice. Some turn to food as an outlet, while others experience depression and refrain from eating the daily recommended calories.

The methods people choose to use to help them cope with the issues life brings their way can either be helpful or harmful to their future existence.

The method I used in times past to cope with the trials life brought my way could hardly be called a method at all. At the onset of a problem, I would discuss it with the person with whom the problem existed in hopes of finding an amicable and reasonable solution that would prove satisfactory to all parties involved. However, in some instances, talking was- to put it simply- a waste of time.

From dealing with people on a daily basis, I have learned that once a person's mind is made up and his/her perception is fixed, it is hard to change his/her mindset. Of course, this is not true of all persons, but it is for most. As a result, I chose to not waste valuable time by beating a dead issue.

After learning that my old method was not as successful as I would have liked, I began to immediately move toward a solution without a lot of discussion, so the problems could be properly dealt with but with less headache. It is not to say that I moved toward a decision hastily. It means that once I had thought the problem over, I moved toward action rather than talking to people who are close minded. In doing so, I became accustomed to just putting out fires without allowing myself to deal with the emotional ramifications that arose from the fires. I refrained from entering into discussions with people who could care less about my viewpoint or the way I felt about the issue at hand. I did not discuss my feelings with them. I learned to tuck them away.

However, I failed to realize the therapeutic nature of discussions. I focused on the negative aspect- the lack of thought-filled responses from the other party.

Putting out fires successfully is beneficial to one's life as it prevents problems from festering and becoming exacerbated. However, not addressing the emotions one feels or should feel is counterproductive because the feelings get bottled away rather than addressed.

Have you ever seen a bottle that was filled to the rim with water and then placed into the freezer? As the temperature of the water decreases, the water begins to harden. As the water hardens, it causes the bottle to expand and change shape. If the bottle stays in the freezer too long, the cap may be pushed off to allow the ice room to expand, or the bottle itself may crack to allow for expansion.

Let's compare these same effects on a person who has bottled up emotions that have not been attended to. Built up feelings can lead to a hardened heart, which in turn can cause a person to explode. Explosions can manifest in a variety of manners.

One, the person may simply "go off" on those around him/her. We all know someone who is known to have a short fuse. When a person fails to have a healthy outlet, he/she may take on the characteristic of a person with a short fuse. This happens because the person has not let out all that has been pushed down inside and consequently does not have room to take in any more. The only recourse is to let the emotions out. This is potentially hazardous to the individual who is experiencing the pent-up emotions and those who come in his/her path.

Two, the person can have health-related issues, such as an increased stress level that may lead to a heart attack or a stroke. Stress is said to be the number one killer, and it is a silent killer. It will sneak up on a person without any warning signs.

Three, the person may go into complete shut-down mode where he/she is not willing to interact with people on an emotional level at all. This is called protective mode. Rather than sharing one's feelings with others, the person decides to keep them inside. Eventually, they become stacked on top of each other and the burden of carrying the emotions can become unbearable.

Four, the person may have a nervous breakdown due to the unresolved issues. A nervous breakdown is very disturbing and also damages one's self confidence. The person loses the motivation and energy to do things that he/she would perform daily and these seem to be impossible for him/her. A nervous breakdown has an impact on one's work and on personal relationships that leads to concern and worry.

To prevent any of these conditions from being my reality, I have decided to write this book as a means of a healthy outlet. In this book, I will share several incidents with you that have never been shared in full detail before. Some people know of these occurrences, but they do not know the full impact these occurrences have had on my life.

Again, the sole purpose of this book is to render healing unto me and anyone who may have experienced the same situations. This is the method the Holy Spirit gave to me through an evangelist after I heard the word of the Lord through a prophetess in 2010 and a prophet in 2012.

After you read each chapter, you will find a section titled **A Moment of Reflection**. In this section, jot down your thoughts and emotions if the topic is applicable to your life. Writing will create an outlet for you as you read. Also, you can read together with a friend or a reading group and discuss the topics addressed within. This too will allow for your healing and breakthrough in specific areas.

It is very important that we know our emotional state and attend to anything that is unhealthy. For some of you, reading is healing. For others, writing is therapeutic. Some take a swim, while others take a jog. Whatever your method of therapy is, do it. Allow the Lord to lead you to become the healthy person you are designed to be, so you can be effective in doing what God called you to do.

As the Dust Settles

The Loss of a Matriarch

In Honorable Respect for My Mother

Gloria L. Harrison

"It is appointed unto men once to die."

Hebrews 9:27

As the Dust Settles

The Christian's Goodnight
Sarah Doudney (c. 1871)

Sleep on, beloved, sleep, and take thy rest;
Lay down thy head upon the Savior's breast;
We loved thee well, but Jesus loves thee best
Good night! Good night! Good night!

Calm is thy slumber as an infant's sleep;
But thou shall wake no more to toil and weep;
Thine is a perfect rest, secure and deep
Good night! Good night! Good night!

Until the shadows from this earth are cast,
Until He gathers in His sheaves at last;
Until the twilight gloom be over past
Good night! Good night! Good night!

Until the Easter glory lights the skies,
Until the dead in Jesus shall arise,
And He shall come, but not in lowly guise
Good night! Good night! Good night!

Until, made beautiful by love divine,
Thou, in the likeness of thy Lord shall shine,
And He shall bring that golden crown of thine

Dr. Cassundra White-Elliott

Good night! Good night! Good night!

Only Good night, beloved not farewell!
A little while, and all His saints shall dwell
In hallowed unison indivisible
Good night! Good night! Good night!

Until we meet again before His throne,
Clothed in the spotless robe He gives His own,
Until we know even as we are known
Good night! Good night! Good night!

Just when I had everything going for me, and I perceived all was well...

In 2010, around the month of May, someone said to me, "You need a healing." I believe I was at a conference. When the words were spoken, my godmother who was sitting next to me said, "Um hum," in a state of agreement, more to herself than anyone.

The person who spoke the words to me did not bother to explain what he/she meant. My godmother who agreed with the statement did not bother to explain either.

At the time, I disregarded the statement as a 'statement of the obvious' because I believed the person was picking up my emotional grief and state of bereavement in the spirit.

Just a few months before, on March 7, 2010, I had lost my 57-year-old mother to arteriosclerosis, which is the hardening of the arteries. My mother's death on that Sunday evening came as somewhat of a shock. I carefully say 'somewhat' because although the Holy Spirit had told me her time on earth was short due to her deteriorating health condition, I did not expect it to be at that specific moment in time.

I remember the day like it was yesterday. On the Friday prior, my husband and I along with two of our friends had left for a weekend in Vegas. On that Sunday, we returned home at approximately three or four in the afternoon.

That evening, my husband and I were in our shared home office watching a movie. As I lay on the floor watching the movie, I fell asleep. Just after ten o'clock that night, my telephone rang. Checking the caller id, I saw that my eldest brother Noah was calling. In the back of my mind I had anticipated his call about a personal matter. My thought was to ignore the call and call him back the next morning because I was half asleep, and I do not prefer to speak on the telephone in that manner unless I believe the call is of the utmost importance.

Nevertheless, I did answer the phone. After saying hello, the only thing I remembered was hearing my brother say, "Mom passed today." The only response I could think to give after sitting straight up was "Whose mom?" That probably sounds like a dumb response, but a more accurate description is- it was a numb response, a response of disbelief. To my query, my brother replied, "What do you mean? You only have one." To this day, I have yet to understand his response. He answered my question as if I had asked him, "Which one of my moms?" I guess we were both dealing with the shock of it all.

Ignoring my brother's retort, I quickly wrapped my mind around what he had said. Through tears, I said and asked, "Ok. What happened to her?" I don't recall what he said. The next thing I remember is the call dropping or the phone disconnecting.

I immediately tried to get to my feet, so I could share the news with my husband who was not in the room at the time. I began screaming my husband's name.

As I made my way out of the office door, which is located at one end of the house, and began to make my way into the living room, my phone rang again, but I didn't hear anything on the other end. At that time, I was in the living room, and I was crawling trying to get to my bedroom. I was crying very hard and yelling out my husband's name. He was in our bedroom at the opposite end of the house. When he finally heard me, I had made it to the bedroom door.

As I attempted once again to get to my feet, he grabbed me to keep me from falling as I said, "My mom died. My mom died." In my state of oblivion, all of this occurred with my seventeen-year-old son in the house. I gave no thought to him finding out in that manner that his maternal grandmother had passed. I would have preferred to have sat down with him and told him in a much calmer manner.

But as we know, life cannot be planned instance by instance. Many times, our lives are dictated by circumstances that are beyond our control. These situations show us how little control we have. God has always had and will always have all power. He permits us to have a limited amount of power and influence over some things.

As I stood in the doorway of my bedroom telling my husband about my mom, I believe I heard my son's bedroom door open behind me. He walked into my room with a questioning look on his face as if to ask, "What is going on?" I just looked at him and said, "Punkin died."

All of my mother's seven grandchildren (at the time) called her Punkin, rather than any of the traditional grandmother names. When my mother's first grandchild Quantanique Shanté Williams was born, my mom decided her name would be Gamma. As Gamma began to interact with her first grandchild, she would call her *Punkin.* But one day, all of that would change. Quantanique looked at Gamma, pointed her little finger and said in her baby language, "No, *you* (are) Punkin." From that point on, Gamma's name had been changed to Punkin.

Back to the story of my mom's passing. After I broke the news to my seventeen-year-old son, he turned and walked back into his room and shut the door. In my state of grief, I didn't think about consoling him or if he even needed to be consoled.

My phone began to ring again. Noah was calling back to ask me if I could call Rod, my brother who is two years younger than I am. I consented through my tears and heavy sobs. While trying to breathe, calm myself down and see through my tears, I dialed my second brother's telephone number. I began by asking him where he was and if he could talk. He was out and about with his wife, son and extended family. I made sure he wasn't driving. I shared the news with him. I told him I didn't really have any information except our older brother had found our mother dead when he arrived home that night.

After completing the call with Rod, I prepared to drive an hour to my brother's home where my mother was residing. The coroner's office had not yet arrived although all other medical and police personnel were on the scene. I told my brother to not allow them to remove her body before I arrived. I needed to see her.

As my husband drove, we both were quiet except when I would start crying again. It seemed so surreal. I kept asking myself over and over again, "How can she be gone?"

When I arrived, the coroner's van was there, and Noah and the youngest of my three brothers August were standing outside. When I saw August, I felt his pain as the youngest child, and I began to cry again. When I saw Noah, I hugged him and began to sob rather loudly. My brothers and my husband assisted me into the house. At that point, I thought I would fall. Carefully, I made it to the restroom to clean my face. I was gagging and coughing, which was a result of my heavy crying.

After cleaning my face, I was able to say hello to my uncle, aunt (one of my mother's older sisters) and cousin who were all there.

I could not even imagine what my aunt was going through. My mother had been her traveling partner. My aunt was the last one who had spoken to my mother earlier that day in the mid-afternoon at approximately two o'clock. My mother was the first of her nine siblings to pass, not including Claretta, my grandmother's tenth child, who died as an infant. Although everyone knew of my mother's heart condition, I am sure no one expected her to be the first to pass because she was the third youngest of the nine. Only God knows the date and the hour of our births and our deaths.

After sitting with my family in my brother's living room for what seemed like hours, the coroner was finally ready to bring my mother's body downstairs. During the wait, I had many, many thoughts of acting as a rebel rather than the dignified person I have been trained to be. I wanted to break all the rules and run upstairs and see and hold my mother in my arms. As I sat on the couch, my heart was breaking knowing she was upstairs alone without me. I felt that she needed me to be there with her and to not leave her alone with strangers who were undoubtedly poking and prodding her body.

Although I was having those thoughts, I knew my mother was not upstairs. I knew that she was comfortably resting in the bosom of the Lord. The word of God says in 2 Corinthians 5:8, *"that we are willing to be absent from the body and to be present with the Lord."* My mother's eternal resting place is without question in my mind. I had seen her life on a daily basis as she raised me from the time she bore me at the tender age of sixteen until I graduated high school and left for college.

Just like all of us, she did some things that God frowned upon, but her heart was fixed on Him. She loved and honored the Lord and committed her life to Him. She would not have had it any other way.

Finally, someone from the Coroner's Office asked us to step outside while they brought her body downstairs. My family and I stepped out onto the front porch and lawn. We made idle chit-chat, but mostly we were quiet. After about thirty minutes, I was able to see my mom. She was laying in a body bag on a gurney with only her face exposed. Her mouth was slightly ajar, and she appeared to be sleeping. I immediately went over to kiss her. The chill of her skin confirmed that she was no longer housed in her earthly body. Without question, my mother had departed this earth realm earlier that evening without me having an opportunity to say 'goodbye' or 'I will see you on the other side.' Again, it seemed so unreal that I was saying goodbye to her at that moment.

After the coroner closed the bag and began to wheel her out of the hourse, I followed behind them. It was almost as if I did not want them to take her. Maybe I wanted to keep her a little longer. But the rational part of me didn't say a word. I just followed. My husband attempted to stop me from following the coroners. He said, "There's nothing more you can do. She's gone." I pulled my arm from his grasp and said, "I want to watch them put her in the van. I want to make sure they are careful with her." I would have been remiss in my duties as a daughter if I had not done so.

When I returned back inside the house, I immediately went upstairs to her room. Her bathrobe was lying on her bed. I immediately claimed it for myself. I just wanted something of hers, so I could have her close to me, and so I could smell her scent. Earlier that evening, there was a bag of jewelry that was lying on the dining room table. It was the jewelry that my mother was wearing at the time of her passing. The coroners had removed from her body. I selected a silver butterfly ring. My mother was an incessant butterfly lover. I placed the ring on my hand, and it has remained there since the time of her passing. I will never part with it. It is my memento.

The next week that led up to the funeral services was difficult. On that Monday, the day after my mom's passing, I went to work and taught my classes. By Wednesday, I needed to take off. I was responsible for putting my mother's obituary together. Reading and typing everyone's words and thoughts was emotionally draining.

I thank God that my brothers and I worked cooperatively during this process. We had no problems whatsoever. Noah and I took the lead as the eldest two siblings, and Rod and August did their respective parts.

On the Friday prior to the funeral service that would take place on the next Monday, we had a private wake. That was my mother's strict instructions. She wanted a closed-casket service. She was adamant about not having anyone looking at her. So, for the wake, only family members were allowed to come to view the body.

When I walked into the chapel room that held her casket, I slowly approached the casket. My reaction was so unexpected, especially to myself. I surprised myself. When I saw her, I immediately bent forward as if I would fall and began to sob. I had to leave the room. I found a chair in the hallway and cried. Thank God my godmother was there. She attempted to comfort me, but I still felt so alone without my mother. What was I to do?

On the day of the funeral, I was very much an active part of the service. This was strictly by choice. As a person who officiates services and is usually asked to speak at one point or another in a service, I could not and would not sit at my mother's home going service and not utter a public word. If someone was going to say something, it would most definitely be me. I would have sorely regretted it if I had not.

During the service, I shared words about my relationship with my mother and a few things that she taught me that impacted my life. I sang with the choir, and I shared my neice's words of love because the US Air Force would not release her to come home as she was currently deployed to Kuwait.

At the end of the chapel service, before going outside to the graveside for the final part of the service, my brothers and I walked with our children up to my mother's casket. My sons, one in each side, were crying very hard. I was able to give them comfort and walk them into the hallway that led outside. Afterwards, I began to walk up to all my minister and pastor friends who came to support me. My intent was to thank and hug each one.

However, when I reached my big sister-in-Christ Evangelist Neldra Davis, my knees buckled and all my emotions came pouring forth. I cried so hard that the tears blinded me, and I could hardly breathe. Everything was a blur. I heard someone telling my husband to hold me. He responded adamantly, "I have her." I heard someone else say, "Give her some air. Move back."

Once I was placed in a chair, near the casket, all I could see was the funeral directors taking the flowers from the top of the casket, so the pallbearers could prepare to carry it out. Then, one of the funeral attendants brought me a bottle of water. I kept my eyes on the casket. Finally, I jumped up and ran to Bishop Leon Martin. He hugged me tightly and told me to be strong. The truth of the matter is- I didn't want to be strong. Being strong on a daily basis and not releasing causes me to constantly find myself in the situation where I need an emotional healing. I need to know that it is okay to cry and that it is okay to release.

After I collected myself, my brothers and my cousins, who were all serving as active pallbearers, carried my mom's casket outside to the hearse. Wanting to be nearby, I followed closely behind the casket. I was almost close enough to touch it. I actually wanted to. If I had given it any thought prior to that day, I would have requested a pair of white gloves, and I would have been the seventh person to assist with the casket. I would not have carried it, but I would have officially walked behind it with my hand lying on the top.

After getting into our cars and driving around a few curves and re-parking, we arrived at the grave site. There, we had the second part of the service. I read a poem that my second brother Rodney wanted to have read. Next, we released butterflies in my mother's honor. There was one butterfly in particular that did not want to fly away. It landed on the lapel of my white blouse and stayed there for quite some time.

Dr. C reading a poem during the release of the butterflies. Look where one landed.

At the end of the graveside service, my brothers and I, along with my sons, some of my nephews and an uncle or two, used shovels and placed the first earth onto my mother's casket. Some of us also threw flowers into the grave.

Aaron M. White, Sr. (front) and Noah A. Williams, Sr. (rear) placing fresh earth on the casket.

Dr. C tossing roses onto the casket.

Finally concluding the service, we thanked our extended family (my mother's siblings, our cousins, etc), our friends, and my mother's co-workers (both past and current) and friends for coming. We took a few photos and departed. Some of our family and other guests went to my home church for the repast. There, we enjoyed each other's company and officially closed out the funeral service for my mother Gloria Louise Harrison on March 15, 2010.

Noah, Sr.; Qua'Nico; Nic; Maurice; Paul; Tye; Vanessa; Dr. C; Rod; Jerithea; August
(from left to right)

Words of Wisdom- When you have lost someone who was close to you, allow yourself time to go through the grieving process. Death is a part of life. Sometime during our lives, we all will experience the death of a loved one. By the same token, there will be loved ones who will experience our death.

Note- each person grieves differently. While some may not understand your grieving process, you may not understand theirs. That is not important. What is important is you allow yourself time to grieve. This is not a process that can be rushed. Take as much time as you need, and do not let anyone rush your process.

A Moment of Reflection- Dealing with Death

If you have ever lost a loved one, answer the following questions.

Write the name of your loved one and the nature of your relationship. Explain how you felt at the time of your loved one's passing. How do you feel today? Have you been able to talk about your loved one's death to others? If you have, how did you feel after you spoke about the incident? If not, what prevents you from sharing what happened and how you feel about it? Do you feel you permitted yourself time to grieve? Why or why not?

_____
_____
_____
_____
_____
_____
_____
_____
_____
_____
_____
_____
_____
_____

As the Dust Settles

As the Dust Settles

The Friend who Became a Client

A Learning Experience

"A righteous man is cautious in friendship, but the way of the wicked leads them astray."

Proverbs 12:26 NIV

This Is Our End
© Jessica A. Phillipi

You can stand there and smile you can sit there and laugh

but you can't trick me I know it's a mask

You're trying to lie to me and everyone else

but why is it that you're lying to yourself?

You can calmly sit there and try to look cool

but I know your emotions and I know you're a fool

I know inside you your feelings rage

The suspense builds with the turn of a page

By day you're one person by night another

and neither of them have anything to do with each other

I've watched you sink farther from your heart

and all of this just tears me apart

I sit here and cry, for you not for me

What you've become I wish you could see

No words could I use to help me explain

what it does to me to see you in pain

You're not there anymore my dearest friend

I hate to say this but this is our end

Dr. Cassundra White-Elliott

Starry Nights
© Malary

Buried underneath

These lies you tell

These games you play

I lie awake

Suffocate

Staring up at a sky that's grey

Play dumb

Bite my tongue an play along

Humming to your every word

Like the tune to my favorite song

Well the time is today

For these clouds to fade

Get everything out in the open

An to end this charade

While in the meantime

Holding back what I want to say

Heading down the same road

Feeling the same way

About to explode

Letting it all build up

Not saying a word

Just glazing up at the stars

[Praying someday you will change]

In 2002, I wrote and published my first book. I was very excited about this new dimension that God had brought into my realm of existence. After my first book, I quickly moved into my second book. Since then, I have been forging ahead with my writing and publishing.

Including the book that you are presently reading, I have written and published nearly twenty books. In the interim of writing and publishing my own books, I established CLF Publishing, LLC to be able to publish other persons' books. Even as I sat composing this book, I had several clients' books I was editing and preparing for publication. God has definitely favored my business.

But, as with all other aspects of life, everything is not always peaches and cream. We must remember, in the middle of the fleshly, juicy peach is a pit that is neither edible nor digestible. In the midst of a cherry, a deep red sweet fruit, is also a pit that must be discarded. Along those same lines, many women adore red roses, especially those with the long thick stems. However, if one is not careful when handling a rose, he/she may have a small amount of blood drawn from the fingertips as a result of being pricked by the thorns that have grown on the stem.

I use all of these illustrations as analogies to illustrate the unexpected difficulties and small pricks one can encounter during the span of a lifetime.

Having passed the milestone of forty years of age, I am quite adamant about living a drama-free life. I understand difficulties will arise and small fires will need to be extinguished here and there. But, I do not plan to need to call an entire fire department to come to my rescue for any given situation.

However, I have learned in this business of publishing, there are clients from varying backgrounds and mentalities. The account I am about to share is an incident that truly rocked my publishing and personal world.

This account is being shared for one purpose and one purpose only: to render health and healing to my heart and yours, if you should have a run-in with a friend. It is not my intent to bash or harm, but to be free. For that purpose, I will share the details of the account, but I will not reveal the identity of the person. For the ease of telling the story, I will call her Carmen. This is the case of the friend that became a client.

Before I get into the actual incident, allow me to provide a brief background of our friendship. Carmen and I met at our church. However, for reasons to be left unwritten, we never developed a relationship until years later. We were connected through a mutual friend who was also a member of our church. As time would have it, the three of us began to work in ministry together and were often referred to as The Three Musketeers. This continued for a span of seven years off and on even though the three of us no longer attended the same church.

During that time, Carmen approached me about publishing her book, but nothing ever came of it. From my understanding, she sought out other publishers. And, I assumed she was going to have one of them publish her book. However, one day out of nowhere, Carmen and I saw one another at my church; afterward, we went to lunch, along with my husband and some of the other church members. While standing in line to place our order, Carmen began to talk about her book and her book signing event that would take place in four months.

I was excited Carmen had progressed with her book and was moving toward publication. From the conversation we were having, I assumed she had a publisher and her book would be going to print soon. So I politely asked, "Who is your publisher?" She giggly responded, "Hopefully, my sister." In a fog, I said, "Who?" She answered, still giggling, "You."

Before I consented, I asked, "Your book signing is in a few months and the book is not yet being published? Don't you think that's a little backwards?" She responded, "No, I'm going to get it done." From that conversation, I should have run and run quickly. Her situation was a classic example of placing the cart before the horse. Her method of planning should have let me know that she was not the most detail-minded person when it came to making a complete plan. Did that register in my mind? Yes, it did. But, did it prepare me for the battle to come? Not hardly!

Let me say this. I had plenty of interactions with Carmen before to have known that I should have been aware, but I thought if I carefully and patiently explained the process to her and all I needed for her to do and when, all would be well. Can someone say, "Wishful thinking"? All my talking, explaining, and complaining were all in vain.

So, this is what happened. As I like to say- **the plot thickens!**

When Carmen and I stood in the restaurant talking, the month was March. We discussed her submitting her book to me at the beginning of April. She stated she had another chapter or two to write and a month would be sufficient time to write.

During that time, my church was planning a women's retreat. The next week, I asked if she was interested in going. She said, "Yes. That will give me a quiet place to write." A red flag went up. The flag caused me to ask, "How is it that you will be writing on April 19 and 20 at the retreat if you plan to give me the book on April 1?" To my query, she did not provide a solid answer. She simply stated, "Just in case I'm not done I can use the retreat as an opportunity to write."

To move the story along, the date was pushed back to May 1, which would be two and a half months before the pre-scheduled book signing. On that date, the prescheduled payment would also be rendered. May 1 came and went. On May 3, Carmen and I met from 7pm until 1am on May 4. I gathered all parts of the book from her computer and transferred them to mine. However, the scheduled payment was not made.

My normal procedure for publishing is to have all clients submit their documents electronically, which usually means email submission. However, because Carmen was a friend and is not computer savvy, I tried extra hard to give leniency. This too was another mistake. When Carmen arrived at my home office, she brought her laptop and a flash drive. She showed me all of the documents that pertained to her book. By the time I finished copying the files onto the flash drive, there were forty-eight documents total instead of just one.

When I began to open the documents and survey them, most of them did not have a specific title. The title of the file mostly corresponded with the first sentence of that document. There was very, very little sentence structure and no paragraph breaks whatsoever. There was also no indication as to which of the forty-eight sections was to go first in the book, second, third, etc. This is why our initial meeting took six hours instead of only the standard one hour.

Immediately, I had to come up with a plan of action. I began to print all forty-eight sections of the book. While the pages printed, I asked Carmen about the table of contents because I did not see one amongst the forty-eight sections. In response to my question, she only gave me a blank stare. I asked her if each of the forty-eight sections was a chapter. To this query, she easily answered, "No. Some of them go together."

I located a few blank sheets of line paper, and I asked her to form a table of contents. As she did so, I continued to print the remainder of the forty-eight sections and stapled each set together. After the table of contents was completed, I gave her the set of forty-eight sections and asked her to label each section by the chapter it belonged to. At that point, she had included twelve chapters on her table of contents.

I am pointing out the details because I want to illustrate the amount of work that needed to be done in a two and a half month time frame. And what is also important to note is although the book signing was two and a half months away, I did not have the full time for publishing. Time also needed to be allowed for printing, which generally takes two to three weeks. This decreased my working time to seven weeks.

Prior to Carmen's submission of her manuscript, she continually asked, "How long will it take you to read and edit the book?" I would consistently tell her, "It depends on the length of the book and how well you write." She could never tell me how long her book was, and I had never read any of her writing. So, the best I could tell her was approximately one month.

I also let her know that payments need to be timely or production would cease. I thought this arrangement was more than fair, especially when I was only charging her for publishing, ISBN assignment and the pictures that needed to be purchased for the interior of her book. I was blessing her with free editing, which in the end totaled $3500 alone. Come on, say it with me- MISTAKE!

There are some people you cannot do favors for because the more you give, the more they expect and want. I personally do not share that mentality. I believe anything I want or need, I can pay for. However, if someone wants to bless me, praise the Lord! But, I do not walk around with the mentality that everything should be given to me free or at a discount. Instead, I look to be a blessing to others. In return, I am truly blessed by God.

Let me make this clear- at the time that I was engaged in publishing Carmen's book, publishing was not my full-time job. I had not begun to dedicate the majority or even half of my time to it. Teaching was still my primary career. At the time, I taught for two community college colleges and two universities. This clearly shows I did not have all day to dedicate to her book, but with the condition it was in, I had to stay up late and get up early for over two months to get it done.

Back to the story...

After Carmen, labeled all forty-eight sections with numbers 1-12 for the respective chapters, she informed me that there were yet portions of the book that still needed to be typed, but it would take no more than a week to get the remaining sections typed and to me.

Having been presented the book information, I developed a plan. I decided once Carmen submitted her first full payment and the remaining information for the book, I would print out the book, place the pages in a three-ring binder, and give it to her, so she could read the entire book from beginning to end. I was quite adamant about this because I knew she had not read the book in its entirety in book form because it was not in a single document on her computer. There is no way that she went from one document to the other reading from beginning to end.

Having Carmen read the book through before I began to edit would eliminate problems down the road. To make a long, long, long story a little less long, I'll say this- it did not happen.

The next day, in the evening, I was asked to come by and pick up the first payment. I did, but to my non-surprise I did not receive the full payment. The payment was a little short. Although it was only a little short, I refused to move toward working on the book because I was working in the capacity of

As the Dust Settles

my business and not my friendship although I had clearly let our friendship affect the business relationship.

When I picked up the payment, I was asked about the print out of the book that would be placed in a three-ring binder. The only thing I could say in the midst of my fury was, "The agreement has not changed." All the way to my next destination, I wondered what I had gotten myself into. Everything in me wanted to walk away. But no! I had to be so willing to help.

The next day, I received a voice message that was strictly professional in tone. When I returned Carmen's call, I was asked to clarify what the arrangement was about the money and my getting started. I restated my terms. I was to pick up the remaining portion of the payment the next day. However, that did not happen.

A few days later, a tragedy struck Carmen's family. At that point, I thought the book would be put on hold which would be perfectly understandable. However to my surprise, Carmen said, "No. I must press forward." However, there was nothing for me to do because the remaining portion of the first payment had not been rendered.

One week later, the same type of tragedy struck my family. Then, three days later, tragedy struck again: three deaths: one in Carmen's family and two for me.

As we both dealt with our heartbreak and heartache, we prepared for funerals.

In the interim, Carmen's family needed money, so she sent me a text and stated if I was not working on her book, could I return the money she had given to me. Her request caused several thoughts to run through my mind. Some of the thoughts included: 1. Really! What does she think? That I have the money sitting in a drawer somewhere. 2. I don't have it, but God will provide. 3. I knew something would go wrong with working with her. 4. No problem. Let me give the money back and walk away. Good riddens, and she better not call back to restart because I will simply refuse. 5. Why not just ask me for a donation on a personal level? Why keep mixing business and personal together?

After receiving the text message and calling to confirm a time to drop off the money, I went into my office to work. Later, I would go and deliver the money. This was the second time disappointment within the project hit me.

When the time came to get dressed and take Carmen the money, I noticed she had called since the time we had spoken earlier. When I returned her call, I heard the unexpected. After her first call to me, one of her daughters gave her a revelation by saying, "Mom, don't have Dr. Cassundra give you the money back. If anything you should be giving her the rest of the money. I will give it to you to give to her."

Carmen proceeded to tell me that the devil was playing with her mind and trying to rear up his ugly head and cause division. She said we both were dealing with our tragedies and we should come together as sisters. She continued by telling me she loved me and she wanted to see me because it had been a while since we had seen each other.

I went to her place of business, collected the remaining portion of the first payment and made small talk, all with a confused heart. Just when I thought I would be released from the assignment of publishing her book, it was not to be so.

Due to the change in life's circumstances, the plan to provide Carmen with a complete print out of the book for her perusal before I began editing and the plan for her to type the remaining portions of the book in a week's time would never come to pass.

At that point, Carmen suggested we create a plan B. The plan included my going ahead with the editing while she made funeral arrangements. Note- at that point, more than two weeks had elapsed from the time she had given me her manuscript and the partial payment. Therefore, I had five weeks left to pull the book together.

I proceeded to edit the document. This is when I learned how much work needed to be done to prepare the document into a coherent and viable manuscript.

Day by day, I placed my efforts into Carmen's book. At various points in the editing process, I printed pages and delivered them to her with questions that I needed to have answered to provide clarity about what had been written.

However, each time I submitted a set of pages to Carmen, I would have to beg and plead with her to read the pages and address the highlighted and bolded portions.

At that stage, the funerals had all passed, and each of us was able to give our complete attention to the book. However, this perspective was held by a single person: me. By the lack of feedback I received, it was obvious that Carmen did not share my perspective.

On two occasions, we did meet to address my questions and concerns. However, the meetings needed to be more frequent, and new concerns continued to arise. The more of the book I read, the more clarity I needed. Having more frequent meetings did not occur, so I forged ahead the best I could.

As I neared completion of the editing process and the formatting of the book, I called Carmen to ask her if she had the money for me to purchase a portion of the pictures she desired to have in the book. Her response would have led a person to believe that I was asking her for money that was going into my pocket. She said, "I have other things I need to do. I have bills I need to pay. But if you just have to have it, I can probably get it." I promptly replied, "Hold on! I don't just have to have anything. This is your book; it's up to you when you want the book done. I am in the middle of formatting your book. You keep asking me how long the book is and how much the printing will cost. I cannot give you an accurate answer if I don't know how long the book is. When I add the pictures, the book will become longer. And, I still need the other pictures from you that you want in the book. I have yet to receive those." To say the least, I was hot!

That same day, I stopped by Carmen's place of business to see someone who was there, and Carmen voluntarily paid the money for her pictures without me bringing the topic up. However, when it came to the other pictures for her book, she requested I go onto Facebook to get the pictures rather than supply them herself. Searching the various Facebook sites only took more valuable time.

This was just another stumbling block to the completion of her book. From my perspective, Carmen wanted to complete the process the way she wanted to complete the process rather than take instructions from me. At one point, I was so fed up that I sent her an email explaining the difficulties I was having. Did the email change her patterns? No!

As we neared the date the book was to be sent to print, Carmen made her final payment for publishing and began to put together the money she needed to pay for printing. At that time, however, she had not yet submitted the additional portions of the book she had mentioned during our initial meeting in the beginning of May.

On one Sunday afternoon, after church service had ended, my husband and I sat waiting for Carmen to arrive to our church, so we could travel home together. The day before, she had requested to ride home with us; I consented and provided her with the time we were expected to depart from the church. She arrived two hours later. My husband and I were both beside ourselves with fury. She was already not on my good side, and this episode did not help.

Once we arrived to our city of residence, we proceeded to go to my home rather than dropping Carmen at her home. It was my plan to keep her in my company, so I could get the answers to the questions I had about her book. Once I was satisfied, she would be free to depart.

After we took an inordinate amount of time working on the book, I finally had the answers I sought for all the highlighted and bolded portions that were unclear. However, to my dismay, I was informed that I would get yet another set of inserts for the book. The original set of inserts I had been waiting a month and a half for had been given to me, but there was much confusion about the material. As a result, much conversation ensued.

The problem with receiving another set of information was the hour within the book completion was late and far spent. The next day, which was a Monday, her book was due to be sent to print. With all that was yet going on, it would take a miracle for that to transpire. Prior to the close of the Sunday meeting, I firmly stated, "I am going to get up at 6am to do a final read-through of your book. Whatever material you have that needs to be inserted must be sent to me by midnight tonight. Do you believe you will get finished typing by then?" Her answer came back affirmative.

Based on how the reading/telling of how this story is going, I am sure you already anticipate the disappointment that was about to fall on me once again.

Later that night at about 9:30pm, I received a text asking if she could have until six the next morning to send the information. She stated she had nowhere to send the information from because she did not have Internet access at home. She would be required to go to Starbucks the next morning to use the Internet. How could I possibly agree to someone having a deadline at the same time I needed to begin the final read through? From that conversation, amongst my fury, I had to resolve in my spirit that the deadline would not be met.

The problem was larger though. That Monday, I was scheduled to leave town, and I would be gone until Thursday. On Friday, I would be leaving again and not returning until Sunday. That meant I would not be able to work on her book for another week.

I had shared this information with Carmen. Therefore, one would expect for the impacted person to do everything in her power to not have to experience the impact of a week's delay. Maybe that is just my train of thought.

Needless to say, the information Carmen wanted inserted into her book was not submitted to me until 1:30pm (not 12 midnight as I requested and not 6am as she had later requested) when Carmen arrived at my home office. Once again, I was required to place the information from her computer onto her flash drive and then onto my computer. This process took approximately one hour because Carmen had to locate the files on her computer. Then, she had to locate the exact locations within the book that the inserts needed to be placed.

This particular Monday was three weeks before the scheduled book signing. Also, this was the day her book was scheduled to be sent to print. However, with the inclusion of the inserts, there was no way I could edit the four new sections, re-read the surrounding sections for flow, edit the table of contents, reformat the book as needed, and send it to print at that late hour in the day. Nor did I feel I should be pressured to rush due to someone else's negligence. After all, she was the one with the prescheduled deadline- not me.

At 3pm, I rose from my desk, after shutting down my computer, pushed in my chair and said, "Okay, let's go." Carmen looked up at me with a questioning look. I said, "I'm going to pick up my son, drop him off and I am leaving town."

On my way to my son's home, I was asked to drop Carmen off at a friend's home. On the way there, I felt disappointment set in once again. I just did not seem to be able to get through to Carmen about deadlines and procedures.

As we drove, I kept running through my mind the best way to establish an understanding as we were definitely experiencing a lack of one. Due to what had just transpired, Carmen's book would be delayed another week. I was not due to work on the book again until the following Monday. Knowing that day would be fourteen days before her event, I felt the pressure.

While driving, I blurted out, "You must want to have a book signing without any books." Startled, she looked at me with a look that asked, "What do you mean?" I began to answer the look that was directed towards me. I began by asking her what she was thinking. I said, "I do not understand how you can be at your deadline and continue to give me more information to add to your book. What are you thinking?" She elected not to answer. I then asked, "So you just are not going to say anything?" She responded, "What am I supposed to say? Nothing I say will change anything." I replied, "I am trying to understand how you think. You need to say something. I want to know how you think, and I will be damned if I get myself into this situation again." She followed by saying, "Well, I never wrote a book before." I said, "Do not go there. Common sense tells a person to submit the book all at one time and not to continue to add more and more segments." Her response was, "What am I supposed to do if everything is not there?" I explained, "You have two choices: one, either leave the book as is and keep the date for the book signing or two, keep adding material to the book until you are satisfied, but move the date back. You cannot have it both ways."

I went on to explain how her book was monopolizing all my time and how it was one thing for me to give up my personal time and sleeping hours, but it was quite another for her to infringe upon my husband's time. She only stared at me with a blank look on her face as if she had just lost her puppy or her best friend. Once again, I was hot!

A week later, eleven days before the book signing, the book had not gone to print. That afternoon, Carmen and I spoke about her book and completed some last minute edits over the phone. However, I needed to leave to go to work. I asked if she would be available again that evening at 9:30pm. She assured me she would be.

At 10:15pm, I called Carmen after having called at 9:30pm, to see if she was ready to move forward with the final edits. Believe it or not, after my profuse complaints about two sets of inserts being added, Carmen yet had more information to be added in. I was livid, to say the least.

Hour after hour passed. At 2:30am, I had had more than enough of listening to menial changes, her secondary editor in the background, all the house noise, etc., etc. At that point, I disconnected from the call after being told a set of scripture was being sent to me for the final section of the book.

After getting a mere four hours of sleep, I awoke the next day at 6:30am. I wearily walked into my office and turned on the computer. I made final edits and included the set of scripture. Next, I electronically transmitted Carmen's book to print. Finally, I sent an email to her explaining the book had gone to print and if there were any errors, it was due to too many last minute inclusions and a lack of time to re-read the entire manuscript.

After I sent the book to print ten days before the pre-arranged book signing, I only had a sense of relief. I was more hurt by the entire ordeal than anything.

I was scheduled to speak at Carmen's event as the inspirational speaker. I wondered if I could pull it off, not because I doubted by abilities to motivate and inspire. No, I can do that with my eyes close. My problem was I needed a healing before being required to be in Carmen's presence.

As time drew on, Carmen's books were delivered three days before the event as a result of her paying for expedited printing and shipping. I delivered the books two days prior to the event.

Lesson learned- It has been said it is best not to mix business and personal relationships. However, time and time again, we do it in order to be of help to our friends who are in need of our assistance. This situation left me with a bad taste in my mouth as well as being hurt and wounded.

I engaged in this situation because I desire to help others make their dreams become reality- that is the motto of CLF Publishing, LLC. At the same time, I want to be appreciated for my efforts- not used and abused.

My advice to you- To avoid potentially stressful situations and to prevent breakups within family and/or friendships, when working with friends and family in a business capacity, set the guidelines in writing and adhere to them. People who are close to us think they will get special favors because friends and family do favors for one another. However, they must remember that business is business and just as they operate with strangers, they should give you the same respect.

A Moment of Reflection- Doing Business

If you have ever had a business deal go sour, whether it was due to the involvement with someone you know or simply with a client/business partner, answer the following questions.

Explain in detail everything that happened during the business venture with the particular client/business partner. As you describe the details of the event, include how you felt about what happened. Also, include how you think the other party felt. Looking back in retrospect, what could you have done differently? If you could revisit the situation, what would you do differently, if anything, if you were faced with the same situation? How do you feel about the situation today? Do you harbor any negative feelings? If not, how did you overcome any negative emotions you may have experienced? If so, how do the emotions affect your business today?

_____
_____
_____
_____
_____
_____
_____
_____
_____

Dr. Cassundra White-Elliott

As the Dust Settles

Under Duress

Oh, Lord! What Shall I Do?

"But the fruit of the Spirit is love, joy, peace, longsuffering, gentleness, goodness, faith, Meekness, temperance: against such there is no law."

Galatians 5:22-23

Share

Jill Briscoe

When fear sees faith a-coming, when doubt sees truth displayed,
The truth that is in Jesus how can we be dismayed?
When tears are wept in secret, when sorrow's night descends,
Then faith in Jesus' power our sorry soul defends.

When we are busy drowning in a sea of sad despair,
When those we love have hurt us and our soul needs God's repair,
When loneliness o'er-whelms us with an ache that none can touch,
And we're crushed with disappointments and life is just too much.

When danger threatens loved ones, when death stalks near to home,
When war shall rise against us, when panic's on the throne,
Remind us of your promises, renew our hearts in grace,
And help us live in righteousness and truth before your face.

So Jesus be our comfort and remind us in your Word,
That our small voice in the tempest incredibly is heard,
In the heaven you inhabit, in the love land where you live,

And you travel through the universe, your peace to us to give!

So we wait now in this stillness that garrisons our soul,
Yes, we wait with hands uplifted till you come and make us whole,
So when faith sees fear a-coming to fill our hearts with dread,
Oh Lord Jesus great and mighty, will you please kill fear dead!

In May 2005, the Holy Spirit began to speak to me regarding ministry. Up to that point, I had been involved in ministry at my church, but God was calling me into another capacity of ministry. As the Lord led me and instructed me on what was to be done, I tuned my ear to hear what He was saying. Having never been in ministry at this capacity, I wanted to ensure I was being spirit led and not flesh led.

Even with God giving me instructions, a year later, I was still not clear on what role I was to play in the ministry. I began to pray earnestly for clarity. I did not want to go ahead of God and make a misstep. In a vision, I heard God say to me clearly "missionary." Having heard His voice, I began to research the role of a missionary, as I was not familiar with the requirements. In my church, we only have evangelists, ministers, and pastors. Additionally, we have our bishop, who oversees all others.

When I researched "missionary" online, I learned a missionary is one who travels to other territories and lands to do the work of the Lord. However, when I went to speak to my pastor about the ministry the Lord had given to me and how God had answered when I asked Him about my role, my pastor explained that a missionary is basically an evangelist in training.

In June of each year, at my church, the pastor has an annual service where he issues licenses and ordains various individuals as members of the clergy. Prior to our annual service, I received a letter in the mail from my pastor stating I would be licensed that year. I was elated with and by the move of the Lord.

By September of the same year, I had planned the first conference to be held on the third Saturday of the month. Months prior to the actual conference and the detailed planning that ensued, the Holy Spirit told me whom to ask to work in the ministry with me. He gave me the name of four evangelists who would assist me in fulfilling God's vision. The ministry was to be called International Women's Commission, which indicated that we were women who were commissioned to preach the gospel by carrying it from our land to international lands. When I extended the invitations, all four evangelists accepted, but only three actually became involved. As time would have it, there would only be two of them who would hang in there for the next several years.

The first conference was awesome. The move of the Holy Spirit was in the place. There were nearly 100 people in attendance. That was Sept. 2006. The committee of ministers was excited about what God was doing. The guests were equally excited as they witnessed the mighty move of the Holy Spirit. My bishop was present, and he anointed me along with each of the four evangelists.

Over the next two years, the move of the Holy Spirit continued and IWC continued to move from one city to the next, hosting a spring conference and the annual conference. In

2007, it was decided to move the conference from land to the ocean. The conference was held upon the Royal Caribbean cruise ship. We sailed the waters for five days. The conference was held on two of the five days. There were twenty people in attendance.

As time progressed, out of nowhere, tension began to grow within the ministry. The Holy Spirit continued to move and speak to me about the next move of the ministry. I would take what the Holy Spirit gave me to the IWC meetings that were held approximately every quarter. At the meetings, I would plainly explain what was given to me and proceed to ask for input on how to put the entire plan together.

At times, I would not get any feedback. Other times, I would be questioned about the very idea the Holy Spirit gave me. I firmly believe that the Holy Spirit will speak clearly to the visionary. Once the visionary is given the idea, she is to develop the plan to carry it out. God allows each of us to use our creative ability to do what He has called us to do. If we are wise, we do not question Him as to the reason why. We simply do what we are called to do.

At times, I felt I was questioned about what God had given me. Statements such as, "You didn't ask us" were made. All I could think was- I was not asked either. I was only sharing what the Lord had said. Because of this, tension grew and grew. It was said, "We are all in this together." But, some thought they had no say or input. In the back of my mind, I questioned if I was off course and if I had made a great misstep. I had to constantly check myself to see if I was wrong.

I went to my overseer and asked his opinion. I told him all that had been said and done. He clearly stated I was not wrong. He said the people must see the vision and get behind it. As I relived each instance that occurred in the IWC meetings, I thought *I would never say that to my pastor. I would never dare walk into a meeting and tell him, "You didn't ask me this or that."* I am at my church to support my pastor and the vision the Lord gives to him. I do it without question and insult. Whenever I need clarity about something, I ask him privately and with a respectful tone.

The same is true for those in ministry with me. They are not there to overrule me, but to support. The tension was so thick that attitudes flared and words were spoken. I felt horribly disrespected and so did others. Each time a meeting was scheduled, I had knots in my stomach and tension in my back.

BUT, I stood my ground. I would not back down or shut down the ministry- as the enemy wanted me to do. I persevered. This continued from 2008 to 2010. In 2010, IWC prepared to embark upon another cruise. During the planning of the cruise, I once again invited the ministry photographer as well as a musician. Both are male. The question came to me- "Why do you get to decide who is going to come as the photographer and the musician? You decided last year. Why can't we invite a woman?" Then, names started being thrown around. Finally, a pastor's name was mentioned. One I had never heard of. To keep the peace, I consented to her being the guest speaker. Mistake, mistake, mistake! Let me clarify quickly. She brought an awesome word the first day. She is an anointed woman of God. She was not the problem.

When the ministry began, it was stated the evangelists who were connected with the ministry would preach. That is what we are called to do- preach. Up to that point, we had done just that.

Having an outside minister required an honorarium. That money could have been used in house, especially for a small ministry. We not only blessed her with the cruise, but it was insisted that she get a love offering- honorarium.

The comment about the photographer and musician was unwelcomed because I paid for their room out of my own pocket, just as I had done for all entertainment and services rendered unto the ministry. The ministry never had money to cover the bill. Therefore, I did not feel that I needed to ask anyone about who I was spending my money on, especially when I know that whom I had chosen were professionals and worth every dime.

The cruise that took place in 2010 had seventy-five participants. The conference was awesome and well attended. We were able to give out information packets, tote bags with the ministry logo, huge chocolate chip cookies baked especially for them, etc. Most participants purchased t-shirts to wear in our group photo. All was excellent. But the tension was still there. After that trip, each minister went her own way without a word about IWC.

That was over two years ago. Since then, I have had peace of mind. The ministry is still in existence and doing well. Each year, I strive to do greater works for the Lord.

I do not have any hard feelings towards any of the ministers who served diligently with me. I love them all dearly, and we are still close. But, I had to quickly realize that God is not the author of confusion. Therefore, where confusion exists, God does not reside. I needed peace of mind and peace in my spirit. I have it now, and I am so grateful unto God for being the peace in the midst of a storm. He is truly Jehovah Shalom! His word tells me to keep my head uplifted toward the hills from whence my help comes (Psalm 121:1).

Today, for each event that IWC hosts, God sends me willing vessels to assist in carrying out the vision. They do not come to kick against the prick (to stand in rebellion). They come to help and bring glory and honor to God. They come to give as well as to receive.

For example, for the seventh annual conference, IWC traveled across international waters into the Caribbean. We safely landed in Montego Bay, Jamaica. The group of participants included pastors, ministers, and others who love the Lord. During the seven days that we enjoyed the Grand Palladium Resort, the conference was held for a duration of two days. We had an opportunity to minister to ourselves along with our visiting guests from Birmingham, Alabama and London, England.

After the conference, we were able to tour the land, lie upon the sandy beaches, enjoy the locals, and eat good food while enjoying one another's company. Most of all, we were able to praise the one true living God in a foreign land!

To show you how God works and presents peace, one evening after having dinner, my husband and I were sitting at the table with a couple of pastors (husband and wife). The husband looked at my husband and said, "It is awesome to be able to see these two work together in ministry," while pointing to his wife and me. "You don't get to see that too often," he continued, "two powerful women working together."

His comment really spoke to my spirit. He spoke the very words I had always desired to experience while working with the other evangelists. I did not organize the ministry to lord over anyone. The ministry was organized to do God's work. At the same time however, I am the visionary, and the Holy Spirit speaks directly to me. However, my authority was not fully received or respected. This was not always the case. In public settings, it would be said I was the leader, the visionary, etc. etc., but in private meetings, any onlooker would have questioned who was in charge. This was hard to deal with and was emotionally devastating and draining.

Through all the ups and downs, the ministry itself has come out on the winning end. God's word in Psalm 34:19 says, "Many are the afflictions of the righteous, but the LORD delivereth him out of them all." I have been afflicted, but God has prevailed. He has brought me through safely. For that, He gets all the praise, the honor, and the glory.

Words of Wisdom-
1. Do not enter into ministry relationships without prayer and clarity, even when directed to do so by God. The word tells us men should always pray and to pray without ceasing (I Thessalonians 5:17). Therefore, we should find ourselves praying at all times. When God gives us instructions, we should pray about how to move within those instructions. Some things appear easier than they actually are. Note- Apostle Paul travelled when God said to travel. He ministered when God said to minister. Although he was obedient, he was not exempt from experiencing trouble. Therefore, do not become discouraged when doing what God has called you to do. Continue to walk in obedience, and trust God to handle each and every situation.
2. Be sure all parties clearly understand their roles and their expected contributions. If necessary, draw up and

contract and have each contributing party read and sign the contract. In times of trouble, the contract can always be adhered to.

3. Always give respect and respect, hopefully, will be returned. Even when you are not respected, you will have peace when you operate in God's principles even when others do not.

A Moment of Reflection- Serving the Lord

If you have served in any capacity of ministry (helps, administration, teaching, preaching, etc.), and you have been misunderstood or had any difficulties, answer the following questions.

Using detail, recall the event you experienced and how you felt about the experience. Do you believe you played a role in what went wrong? Explain your answer. What role did others play in this scenario that you wish could have been different? What, if anything, did you learn from this experience?

_____
_____
_____
_____
_____
_____
_____
_____
_____
_____
_____
_____
_____

As the Dust Settles

A Mother's Heartbreak

Who Would Have Thought?

"Train up a child in the way he should go: and when he is old, he will not depart from it."

Proverbs 22:6

As the Dust Settles

Mother and Son

Rose Falcone

My son
I am here
I cannot protect you
From the world.

My son
I am here
I can only love you
No matter what

My son
I am here
My love unconditional
On this you can rely

My son
I am here
To guide and to teach you
And now you must fly

My son
I am here
Life can be difficult
I hear your cry

My son
I am here
Changes are painful
Never forget who you are

My son
I am here
Maintain the faith
In yourself and in God

My son
I am here
Self acceptance is yours
Do not fear

My son
I am here

In 2001, James my fifth godchild was born. At that time, four of his siblings were already near and dear to my heart, especially his sister because she is my only 'daughter.' But, James has a special place in my heart because he became my son at the time he was born. The others, I had met when they were teenagers. When James was born, my two natural sons were eleven and eight at the time, so he became my third son.

The day after his birth, his mother expired, leaving all six of her children without their natural mother, but not motherless. They have several spiritual mothers and a church family who love them dearly. Five months after James' birth and his mother's passing, the father of his siblings was killed in a car accident. This left all the children parentless. As a result, the eldest sibling was awarded guardianship. Due to the situation, I asked the eldest child if I could take James and raise him. My request was denied.

As James grew from infancy to toddlerhood, I kept him with me as much as I could. Although I had not given birth to him, he was my baby. That is how I referred to him, and that is who he was.

When James neared five years of age, I asked his guardian, once again, if James could come to live with me. Up to that point, James would only come over on weekends and during my breaks from work, i.e. Spring Break, Christmas and summer vacations.

I wanted him to live with me because I was deeply concerned about his education. Only one of his brothers and sisters before him had graduated from high school (some were not old enough yet). I did not desire for James' destiny to be similar. To prevent this, I wanted to provide him with a positive start. I was also very interested in being instrumental in breaking the generational curse of poor educational habits that has led to poor reading, writing, and mathematical skills. However, my request came back stamped 'Denied."

As time progressed, James moved through kindergarten, first grade and second grade. However, at the end of his second grade year, a red flag of concern was erected. His teacher wanted to hold him back in the second grade for another year. She was concerned about his low reading and math skills.

At that point, the eldest brother came to me and asked if I could take James for the next school year. I was elated and saddened at the same time. I experienced elation because my son would come to be with me full time and receive all he was lacking.

In my statement, I am not at all implying he was not well taken care of. He was. However, he was residing in a house where kids were raising themselves. Although they were surviving, there was much that was needed, such as the nurture that only a mother can give.

I was saddened because I had anticipated this occurrence, and it had come to pass. The first years of one's life, along with the first years of formal education, is when the foundation is lain.

The foundation that James had was substandard, and it was being illuminated in many aspects of his life: education, speech patterns, manners, and behaviors. He was a very loving and respectful child, but there was much honing to be done.

At that time, my husband, myself and two sons vowed we would play our part in bringing James up to where he needed to be educationally and socially. One thing I can say is- spiritually, James was not doing so badly. He attended church weekly and was being taught godly principles. After all, that is where I met his siblings years prior to his birth.

One month before the school year began, James came to reside in my home. There was no written agreement or even a verbal one for that matter about how long he would stay with me. However, I assumed he would be there for at least one year, as it would probably take him that long to get to grade level, if not longer. During this time, we played math games with him and taught him phonics. My heart was grieved by what I saw, and my sons were upset that their little brother was so far behind.

When I took James to enroll him in the local elementary school (the one both my sons graduated from), I had a long discussion with the principal- one educator to another and as a mother to an administrator. After our initial discussion where the principal stated her concerns about holding James back due to his age, her perspective changed once she received his transcripts and tested him.

At first, the principal suggested allowing James to begin third grade and work really hard to bring him up to grade level. This suggestion was based solely on the fact that second graders are seven years old and may turn eight towards the end of the year. However, because James was already eight and would be turning nine before the end of the year, he would be much older and bigger than most of the other students in his class. Although I understood her perspective about him appearing to be out of place and could potentially face ridicule- that was the least of my concerns.

After viewing James' transcripts and seeing the low grades he earned throughout his first and second grade years, the principal concurred with me that he needed to repeat second grade. At the point, he only tested at first grade levels in reading, writing and math. So, for four months (from mid-August to mid December), my family and I juggled our schedules to get James to and from school each day Monday through Friday.

It was difficult for us because I taught classes in a different city from our residence, and sometimes my classes began at 7am while James' school did not begin until after 8am. My husband would leave for work each morning at 4:30am. My second son's school began at 7am (he was a junior in high school), and my oldest son had already graduated high school. Therefore, most of the time, he was not at home. However, only his schedule allowed for dropping off James at school on the mornings when I had early classes. The other days, I either drove him to school or walked with him to get my daily exercise.

In the afternoons, I had to utilize the afterschool program to give us time to pick him up. We did a lot of juggling, but we were glad to do it. It was for a much-needed and worthy cause.

When winter break came, James' eldest brother wanted to pick him up. I thought he meant for Christmas break. He meant for good. I was surprised! I did not see the request coming. James was doing well in school. He was completing and submitting all of his class work and homework assignments, and he was learning a great deal. He was on the path to improvement.

But, I then had to deal with his brother's request. I spoke to several persons about it, and each and every person said I should keep James in my home. However, as I explained to each and every one of them- I had no legal recourse. The bottom line was- James was a son on loan to me.

Needless to say, James did return to me after Christmas break to finish second grade with me and my family. But the devastation that I felt was almost unbearable. I shed tears for nearly a week or two. I felt as though I was involved in a child custody case. There were no harsh words between James' eldest sibling and myself, but I felt deeply hurt by the action that was being forced upon me.

From January to May (when the school year came to a close), I began to emotionally disconnect myself. I began to close myself off in an attempt to not have my dreams and hopes blasted into a sea of despair. (Okay, I am being a bit melodramatic, but the hurt was real.) I did not desire to feel the pain and agony. By May, I had come to terms that James would be returning home to his siblings. I also resolved that the door to my home would not be a revolving door. Once James returned to his home, he could come to visit, but he could not come to live. I still wanted the best for him, but I did not want my world torn asunder.

When James' last day of school came, I had his bags packed with all of his belongings, so when his brother came to pick him up for the weekend, he would have all of his items and would not need to return to get anything. You could say I was washing my hands.

Afterward, it took nearly a year for James to come visit. Emotionally, I was not ready for him to come popping in here and there. However, when he requested to come, I allowed him to, but I did not initiate the visit.

Today, I have moved past the incident emotionally, and the scars have healed. I have learned to be godmother rather than mother.

My greatest disappoint about the entire situation is I do not believe any of my godchildren know how I feel about them. They do not know that they are no different from my two natural sons. I thought in the fifteen years that we have known each other that it would be apparent. However, I guess the reality is they do not know. The 'not knowing' causes a disconnect between us. However, I have learned to live with it and move on. But, I must say, it was a process, and there are still residual feelings.

Words of Wisdom- We must realize that everyone does not always feel about us the way we feel about them. This is true in all types of relationships. In a marital relationship, one spouse may feel stronger for the other than the other does for him/her. In sibling relationships, one sibling may favor a particular one of his/her siblings while the favored one may favor a different sibling. Regardless of this fact, we should still keep our hearts open to love regardless of whether the same intensity of the love is returned. Note- this does not mean it is okay to place ourselves in situations where we are not loved and our love is abused. Make sure your relationship is healthy and do not concern yourself with who loves the other more.

A Moment of Reflection- Relationship Woes

If you have ever experienced disappointment in a relationship and it caused you to distance yourself from the particular individual, answer the following questions.

Describe the relationship you had/have with the individual. At what point in the relationship did you begin to feel uncomfortable? What caused the discomfort? How did you handle the situation? How did the other person respond or handle the situation? What did you learn from the situation?

_____
_____
_____
_____
_____
_____
_____
_____
_____
_____
_____
_____
_____
_____

As the Dust Settles

Dr. Cassundra White-Elliott

Oh, Lord! Hear My Cry!

I Need to Feel His Arms

"Hear my cry, O God; attend unto my prayer. From the end of the earth will I cry unto thee, when my heart is overwhelmed: lead me to the rock that is higher than I. For thou hast been a shelter for me, and a strong tower from the enemy. I will abide in thy tabernacle for ever: I will trust in the covert of thy wings. Selah. For thou, O God, hast heard my vows: thou hast given me the heritage of those that fear thy name. Thou wilt prolong the king's life: and his years as many generations. He shall abide before God for ever: O prepare mercy and truth, which may preserve him. So will I sing praise unto thy name for ever, that I may daily perform my vows."

Psalm 61

As the Dust Settles

Here I Am Knocking

© M. S. Lowndes

Here I am standing
At the door of your heart,
Won't you let me come in
And flood light where there's dark?

For I have been knocking
For such a long time,
Don't leave it much longer
To become a child of mine

I just want you to know
That I love you so much
And can fill your heart within
That once was starved of love

So please don't delay
In responding to me,
For I may not keep knocking
And I have not a key

I will never force you
To open the door,

Dr. Cassundra White-Elliott

It's all up to you, my friend,
To receive me as Lord.

At age thirteen or fourteen, after having been a member of the Church of Christ all my life, I wanted Jesus to be my personal savior. However, I was denied my birthright. I was told by my mother or grandmother (or both) that I was too young to understand what salvation was all about and I should wait until I was older. I may not have known much about walking with God, but I knew that I loved Him and that I did not want to go to hell. I wanted to spend my eternity with Christ, who had come and shed His untainted blood for me. I wanted to serve the One who came and was crucified for my sins. I wanted to be washed clean. I did not want to be a sinner, as I was told that I was. But because I was denied the privilege of being born again and I had to honor my mother and grandmother, I refrained from going to the altar. I was deeply saddened, but I knew that my day would come.

I waited patiently for two or three years. On June 30, 1984, on my sixteenth birthday, when the preacher gave the altar call, I stood up, said, "Excuse me," to my grandmother and walked to the altar with a made up mind. I did not stop to ask permission because I did not want to be denied again. I was sure that I wanted to live for Christ and that I wanted to be saved from my life of sin and that I wanted to lean on Him. Every Sunday, we sang "What Will Your Answer Be?" I was tired of not being able to answer God's call. He was beckoning for me. However, at sixteen, I had no idea what He was calling me to do. I would be lying if I said I knew that God was calling me to speak and write to millions of people, so they could be healed, saved, and delivered. I had no clue. I just wanted to be in His presence and experience His awesome love.

Going Astray

After being in church for twenty-three years faithfully, I began to attend church less regularly. When my husband, my son and I lived in Long Beach, my son and I would travel to Los Angeles to go to church with my grandmother. After my grandmother moved to Ontario, I would only go to church in Los Angeles once in a while. It wasn't the same without her. Then, after my family (my husband, my son, and I) relocated to Ontario in 1992, I went to visit the Church of Christ that my grandmother had located and joined. It was down the street from her home. When I walked in, I was flabbergasted. My grandmother and one man were the only African Americans in the building. She had failed to mention that. Was that an important factor for my salvation? No, of course not, but I had never attended an all-white church. The worship was different, and I was not comfortable. So, after that single visit, I went home never to return. From that point, I decided to find a church that I could attend comfortably. That took about five years.

Returning to the Lord

One day, after getting divorced and becoming a single mother of two sons, I found a flyer on my apartment door. The flyer was for Love, Peace, and Happiness (LPH) Family Church in Rialto. On the front of a flyer was a couple, an African American couple that had smiling faces. I decided to attend the church, but I did not attend right away. After some time passed, I got up one Sunday morning, got my sons dressed, and went to church. When I got there, I found the church relatively empty, and I was informed by Pastor Jacqueline Martin that the service time had been changed to one hour later. She asked me if I wanted to come back in an hour, and I said yes. However, I did not go back that day.

A few months later, I moved from my apartment, which was located west of the church to another apartment located just east of the church. At the time, I was working in the payroll department at Laidlaw Transit, as I was finishing my master's degree. At Laidlaw, I met Mary Jackson. I had known Mary for some time, but unbeknownst to me, she was a member of Love, Peace, and Happiness. She told me that she would be in my area that day because she was going to stop by the Rialto location of her church and she wanted to take me and my sons out to lunch after she left church. I asked her where her church was. When she described it to me, I told her I had been there before and I was planning on going back. So, instead of her coming to pick us up after church, I told her we would go to church and meet her there. Ever since that fateful Sunday, my children and I have been members of LPH. That was fifteen years ago.

The purpose of my sharing my personal relationship with Christ is to focus on the time frame that I 'forsook the fellowship of the saints.' During, this time period, I felt alone. I felt I was without my covering- Christ. I felt naked. My mindset was changing, and I was not living a life that was pleasing to Christ. During that time, I experienced divorce and other life disappointments.

On that Sunday, when I attended Love, Peace, and Happiness with my friend Mary, my heart was rejuvenated, and I felt as though I had returned home- to Christ, my savior. The tears ran down my face uncontrollably. I did not care who saw me crying or going down to the altar; I was overjoyed to be back into the arms of the Lord.

Words of Wisdom- If you are a believer and follower of Christ, any time you find yourself breaking away from your church, stop and ask yourself why. In my situation, I moved away from my church and chose not to make the hour drive each week to attend. There are a number of reasons people leave their churches. For example, it could be due to a lack of spiritual nourishment or an ongoing conflict. Whatever the reason is you must decide if you will continue to attend or find a new church. What you must *not* do is find yourself out of church for an extended period of time. If it is no longer feasible for you to attend your home church, look for a new church home and do it quickly.

Think about this- if you are living in a house and the house becomes unlivable, you would not simply live outside. No, you would find other suitable living conditions. Living outside would cause damage to your physical health. This can be equated to 'living' outside the church. Doing so will impact your spiritual condition. So, if you are currently without a church home, find one today and reconnect with the Lord. His arms are yet open. Remember, He told us in His word that He would never leave us or forsake us (Hebrews 13:5). It is us who leaves Him. But, He is always available when we want to return unto Him. Your life will be more fulfilled and satisfying when you nurture your relationship with God.

A Moment of Reflection- Living a Spirit-Filled Life

If you are a believer and have had a moment away from the Lord, answer the following questions.

What led you to go astray from God? How long did you remain away? Have you entered back into fellowship with Christ and the saints of God? If not, why not? If you have, how do you feel? What advice would you give to others who may be faced with the same dilemma?

_____
_____
_____
_____
_____
_____
_____
_____
_____
_____
_____
_____
_____
_____
_____
_____
_____
_____

As the Dust Settles

Dr. Cassundra White-Elliott

Gift of Salvation for Non-Believers

"For all have sinned, and come short of the glory of God."
Romans 3:23

This section was written especially for non-believers, those who have not accepted the gift of salvation. The gift of salvation saves souls from eternal damnation and is a free gift offered by God himself. John 3:16-18 says, *"For God so loved the world, that he gave his only begotten Son, that whosoever believeth in him should not perish, but have everlasting life. For God sent not his Son into the world to condemn the world; but that the world through him might be saved. He that believeth on him is not condemned: but he that believeth not is condemned already, because he hath not believed in the name of the only begotten Son of God."* This section of scripture tells us God's purpose for giving His son Jesus to the world. The world was in a bad condition. The world was overwrought with sin; the people were living for fleshly desires rather than for God's desires.

As a result of the world's conditions, God decided that He would offer the perfect sacrifice that would save the world from being a place where people were lost and had no hope. He decided that His own son could stand in proxy for the sin-filled world, taking all sin upon Himself.

So Jesus came, born of a virgin, to save this dying world. He walked on this earth for 33 ½ years, doing the work of His Heavenly Father. At the appointed time, He died by way of crucifixion upon a cross at Calvary, on Golgatha's hill. He shed his blood and died for you and for me. Because His blood was pure, it paid the penalty for all unrighteousness and gave those who believe in Him direct access to His father's throne.

Scripture tells us in Matthew 27:51 that the veil of the temple was ripped in two from top to bottom, at the moment that Jesus' spirit left His body. As a result of the veil's removal, we are no longer required to have a high priest make intercession for us. We, as the children of the Most High God, are able to approach the throne God for ourselves, and Jesus sits on the right hand of the Father making intercession for us.

But what is even more miraculous than God offering His own son as the perfect sacrifice was the fact that when Jesus was placed in grave clothes and placed in a tomb, He only remained there until the third day. God would not have it that His son would remain in the heart of the earth forever. In order for people to believe in the awesome power of God and His dear son Jesus, a miracle had to be performed. So, on the third day, after Jesus died on the cross, He was resurrected, demonstrating the omnipotence of God. This very act was the act that would cause people to believe in a god that reigns supreme and holds the power of the universe in His very hands, a god that could save them from themselves.

Today, if you are an unbeliever, you can change your destiny. You can change where you will spend your eternity. Our Heavenly Father gives us the freedom of choice about how we want to live our life here on earth and how we want to spend eternity. In Deuteronomy 30:19, God boldly declares, *"I call heaven and earth to record this day against you, that I have set before you life and death, blessing and cursing: therefore choose life, that both thou and thy seed may live."*

So, dear friend what choice will you make today? Will you spend your eternity with the Creator or will you suffer Hell's eternal flames? Again, the choice is yours. Just as the men aboard the ship who were with Jonah became believers, you too can make a choice to accept the only one and true living God as your god.

If after reading the above passages, you have decided that you want to spend your eternity in Heaven with God, the creator, and His son Jesus, and the Holy Spirit, read through what has affectionately come to be known as the Roman's Road. This is the road to salvation. As you read through the scriptures that comprise the Roman's Road, you will also read the explanation for each scripture so you will have clarity about what you are reading and confessing.

The Roman's Road to Salvation

The road to salvation begins with Romans 3:23 which declares, *"For all have sinned, and come short of the glory of God."* This scripture explains that everyone has come short of God's glory and needs redemption. Then Romans 6:23a states, *"For the wages of sin is death."* Here, we learn that the consequence of living a life of sin is death. Everyone will experience physical death as a result of the sin committed in the garden of Eden, but those who commit themselves to a life of sin will suffer eternal damnation in the lake of fire (Rev. 19).

Continue with the rest of verse 6:23 that says, *"but the gift of God is eternal life through Jesus Christ our Lord."* There is an alternative to suffering eternal damnation. We can accept the gift of salvation by accepting Jesus as our personal lord and savior. Then, Romans 5:8 says, *"But God commendeth his love toward us, in that, while we were yet sinners, Christ died for us."* We are able to receive the gift of salvation because Christ came to earth and shed His blood for us on the cross.

Continue to Romans 10: 9-10 which says, *"That if thou shalt confess with thy mouth the Lord Jesus, and shalt believe in thine heart that God hath raised him from the dead, thou shalt be saved. For with the heart man believeth unto righteousness; and with the mouth confession is made unto salvation."* If we confess with our mouths that Jesus is the son of God, that he came and died for our sins, and that God raised Him from the dead, we will receive salvation.

Finish with Romans 10:13, which states, *"For whosoever shall call upon the name of the Lord shall be saved."* Call upon the name of God by saying these words, **"Lord Jesus, come into my heart and save me Lord. I believe that you are the Son of God who came and died on the cross for my sins. I believe that you rose from the grave. I also believe that you now sit in heaven on the right side of the Father, making intersession for me. I accept you as my Lord and my Savior."**

Now that you have confessed with your mouth that Jesus is the son of God and that He died for our sins and rose from the grave, **YOU ARE NOW SAVED!!!!** You will spend your eternity in heaven.

The next step is very important- you must find a bible-based church that teaches the word of God and confesses the Lord Jesus Christ to be the son of God. Don't delay. Do this immediately. Do not leave yourself open to the enemy. Get connected with the saints of the Most High God and keep yourself covered with the unspotted blood of the lamb.

Here is my prayer for you.

Father God,
I thank you for the opportunity to minister your word to the unsaved, the unchurched, and the uncommitted. Father God, I pray now for the souls who have just received the gift of

salvation. Lord Father, they have opened their hearts to you, and I know that you have received them into your kingdom and written their names in the Book of Life. Father God, I pray that you will touch their lives and show yourself mightily before them. Let their eyes be opened by the scales falling off, allowing them to see clearly.

Father God, I even pray for the backslider, those who have turned away from you after receiving the gift of salvation. You said in your word that you desire that none would perish. So Lord, I send your word to them right now praying that they would confess the iniquity in their heart, repent, and turn from their evil ways, so that they may receive a life of abundance. You said in your word in Matthew Chapter 14, that every knee shall bow before you and every tongue will confess that Jesus is Lord.

Father God, I pray now that we all come under subjection to your word and that we will humbly submit our lives to you. I ask all these things in the name of my Lord and Savior Jesus Christ. Amen, Amen, Amen!!!!

I will continue to pray for your success in your walk with God. Remember, this spiritual walk that you are about to embark on will not be an easy walk, but remember, the race is not given to the swift but to those who endure to the end.

Be blessed with heaven's best. I love you!

ABOUT THE AUTHOR

Dr. Cassundra White-Elliott resides in California with her family, where as an English/Education professor she works for various community colleges and universities. One of the universities she teaches for is the Southern California Branch of the University of Phoenix. There she teaches communication studies.

When writing, she writes with the direction of the Holy Spirit, in an effort to share with God's people all that He has for them.

In addition to teaching and writing, Dr. White-Elliott also serves as an evangelistic teacher. She is also the founder of International Women's Commission, a ministry that serves the needs of the entire person, by attending to healing the mind, body, soul, and spirit.

Dr. White-Elliott holds a Ph.D. in Education, a Master's in English Composition, and a Bachelor's in Education.

Dr. White-Elliott is also the founder of CLF Publishing, LLC. For your publishing needs, go online to www.clfpublishing.org.

Dr. Cassundra White-Elliott

OTHER BOOKS BY THE AUTHOR

(All books can be purchased at www.creativemindsbookstore)

As the Dust Settles

From Despair, through Determination, to Victory!

A lot can happen during a span of 40 years. The life of Dr. Cassundra White-Elliott has been anything but uneventful. From a fun-loving childhood sprinkled with incidents of abuse to a tumultuous young adulthood to a stable, secure adult life, she has experienced a full life, with much more to come. Her story is inspiring and motivating.

If anyone lacks hope, reading Dr. White-Elliott's autobiography will propel him/her into an attitude of "Maybe I can." This attitude, if nurtured and developed, will grow into an attitude of "Yes, I can." Throughout her life, Cassundra has always held in her heart the belief that she could achieve anything that she had a made-up mind to embark upon. She was determined to achieve her heart's desires, doing what God has called her to do. She takes no credit for herself. All the glory goes to God, for He is her driving force. In Him, she lives, moves, and has her being.

Through the Storm

Preview

Through the Storm was duly inspired by the avaricious cloud of depression that decided to hover overhead of my daily existence in the latter part of 2007. Although I found it extremely difficult, I was once again compelled to not be defeated by just another snare that the enemy, the trickster, set for me. Once again, or more appropriately I should say *continuously*, he has exerted pernicious efforts to snatch the very life out of me by causing me to wallow in despair and to believe that I had been overcome by failure when in actuality and all reality, I was just experiencing a temporary set back. During those cloudy days, I had to remind myself daily that even though I was a target of the enemy, I am and will always be a child of the Most High god, Jehovah, who is my rock, my stability.

In my last book ***Dare to Succeed by Breaking through Barriers***, I discuss many barriers people find themselves faced with and the keys to successfully breaking through and overcoming those barriers. However, upon the release of the book, I too found myself faced with barriers, barriers in their multiplicitous form. Just as I reminded my readers, I had to continuously remind myself that one of the benefits of being God's child is the ability to be victorious in all battles, which comes from standing firm and continuing to fight the good fight of faith believing that I am an over comer and a conqueror as told to me in Romans 8:37.

During the midst of these seemingly perilous times, a dear friend gave me a cd by the Williams Brothers. While driving and listening, tears streamed from my eyes as I listened to the words of one particular song, "Still Here." The song says,

Heartaches, I've had my shares of heartaches, but I'm still here
Trouble, I've seen my share of troubles, but I'm still here
Bruises, I've taken my lumps & bruises, I but I'm still here
Loneliness, I've had my share of loneliness, but I'm still here

Through it all I've made it through another day's journey, God kept me here
I've made it through another days journey, God kept me here
Lied on, many times I've been lied on, but I'm still here
Burdens, I had to bare so many burdens, but I'm still here
Dark days, I've had my share of dark days, but I'm still here
Disappointments, I've had so many disappointments, but I'm still here

Chorus
It's by the grace of God, that I'm still here today
He was always there, no matter what came my way
I felt the presence of him, in my time of need
Standing right there, just to seal my faith

Chorus
I made it (I made it)
I made it (yes, I made it)
I'm still here (I'm still here)
A lot of folks say that I wouldn't be here tonight, but I made it (I

made it)
By the grace of God , yall (yes, I made it)
I'm still here (I'm still here)

I have to lay awake in the midnight hour sometimes, tossing & turning (I made it)
All night long (yes, I made)
Have anyone had to lay awake all night long sometime (I'm still here)
Tears in your eyes wandering what the next day was gonna bring (I made it)
God kept has arms around you, yes he did (yes, I made it)
You made through the trails (I'm still here)

Come on let me see those hands in the air
I made it, I made it (I made it)
I made it, I made it (yes, I made it)
I made it, I made it (I'm still here)
Through it all (through it all I'm still hereeee)

To me, every word uttered in this song exemplified both my past and present experiences. But the triumph in it all was the victory that was in my grasp. I knew that I had to praise my way through to a new season.

But before victory was attained, with all the burdens that weighed heavily upon me, day after day I seemed to sink further and further, deeper and deeper into an abyss of depression. I fervently tried to shake it. But to avoid the daily pressures, that my life was consumed with, I would sleep later and later each day, in an attempt to avoid the world at large, which seemed to want to swallow me whole. This continued to the point where I would even turn the phone off to avoid not only the insolent bill collectors but also loved ones. I didn't avoid loved ones because I didn't love them any longer. No, I avoided them because I did not want them to hear in my voice the anguish I was enduring.

The irony of it all, though, was that I believed the word of God, and I knew unequivocally that He had not forgotten me and that he would not forsake me, for He had given me a life of blessings and he had already shown me glimpses of a very bright and promising future.

Dr. Cassundra White-Elliott

Unleashed Anger, Anger Unleashed

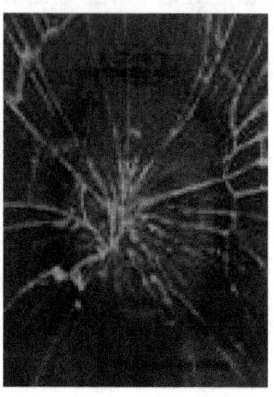

Preview

Introduction

What Is This Book All About?

As I prepared to embark upon the adventure of writing this book, I had to prepare myself to also be transparent. I have found that being transparent is required in order for healing to transpire, healing for all those that peruse the pages of this book and myself. And I may as well tell you that today, at the onset of this project, I have not been totally delivered from my condition of being an anger-filled person. However, I am definitely a work in progress. I have made strides with the assistance of my Lord and Savior, Jesus Christ, who is the head of my life. Without his love, guidance, and teachings, I would not be the woman of God I am today. I shudder to think where I could be instead and will therefore not entertain the thought.

Rather, I will confess that it is my desire that a transformation will result as I do an in-depth exploration of who I started out as when I was a little girl, the woman I became, and the woman that I am striving to be. It is my endeavor to see God tear down walls that encapsulate both my mind and soul and free me from the bondages of anger. It is my prayer that total deliverance will come between the writing of this sentence and the very last one of the book.

So, it is at this point that I must stop and utter a word of prayer.

Oh Heavenly Father,
I just want to stop and take another moment to give you praise, honor, and glory for being just who you are. You are the Alpha and the Omega. You are the finisher of my faith, for you knew my beginning before I departed from my mother's womb and you know my ending as well. Father God, I just want to thank you for your grace, the grace that you have afforded me, oh Lord, to still be here and to be able to tell my story. A story that will set captives free, present company included. Father God, I just want to tell you that I love you because you love me in spite of me. You love me with all my imperfections. You love me because as it says in your word that I am a royal priesthood. I am the daughter of the Most High God; I am the daughter of the King of Kings. Father God, I thank you for your love and the strength to be able to cause this work to come to manifestation. Oh Lord Father, I humble in your sight. I place my face to the ground and cry out your name. I cry out for healing in the name of my Lord and Savior, Jesus Christ. I believe that you will give me favor and grace to heal and to let your glory reign mightily in my life. So, therefore I place my life back into your hands, so that you can do a mighty work. I enter this prayer in the name of your son, Jesus Christ.
Amen.

Readers, as the writing of this book takes me through my transformation, I pray that the reading and re-reading of it will take you through yours. If you desire to be free, as I do, remember freedom can be yours. It is a gift for believers of the Almighty God. We just need to first believe that we can be free, pray for freedom, receive our freedom (by the necessary path as revealed to us by the Holy Spirit), and then confess with our mouths that we are free and are no longer bound.

Dr. Cassundra White-Elliott

Dare to Succeed by Breaking through Barriers

Preview

Introduction

Over the past few years, while conversing with family, friends, associates, strangers and even my students, I have noticed a common pattern amongst believers and non-believers alike. In both groups, there are those who make things happen because of the belief system they live by, and there are others who tend to demonstrate debilitating thoughts about the very course of their lives. Those who demonstrate debilitating thoughts do not seem to believe that their destiny is controllable. They tend to believe that whatever is supposed to happen will happen- on its own. As a result of this type of thinking, they don't put much effort into the outcome of their future, or should I say not as much effort as they could. For non-believers, this attitude and behavior is understandable because some non-believers are driven by their own self will while others have a lack of self will and are, therefore, not driven at all. But for believers who have the word of God, as a guide for their lives, I call this attitude living a substandard life compared to the one that God planned for His children. This is a result of failing to tap into the inheritance that God himself promised believers in His holy word.

Living a substandard life simply means living below one's capabilities. Many people believe that it is the set of talents each of us has been gifted with that enables us to be productive and live a prosperous life. Although our talents and how we use them have much to do with our earthly success and will lend to our prosperity, for believers our talents are not our only resources. God is our source for prosperity and He dispenses it to us. That is not to say that there are not varying levels of prosperity because there are and just like grace it is not dispensed by God evenly amongst men.

However, there are many believers who have failed to tap into the very essence of their beings. They are not tapping into their God-given talents nor are they using the power of prayer to tap into the prosperity that God desires for His children. The bible tells us that, *"the effectual fervent prayer of a righteous man availeth much"* (James 5:16b). When people live below their capabilities, they are not doing everything within their power to live a prosperous and fulfilled life. In many cases, there is one explanation for why we live below our means. Outside of the reasons of just not caring or being unaware of the word of God, in many cases there are barriers that stem from the past that block prosperity and prevent us from moving ahead into the future that God has designed for us.

For non-believers, whatever is in their physical, mental, financial, and educational power is what patterns their lives. Believers, on the other hand, have all these resources available to them with one added bonus. They have the power of the Holy Spirit available to them.

Public Speaking in the Spiritual Arena

Preview

Chapter Two
How Communication Works

Purpose: This chapter will explain the six primary components of communication, identifying their purpose and how they work together.

The Source

In oral communication, the source of information is the speaker. In a church setting, the foundation of the message is God's word, but it is a speaker's interpretation of God's word that is delivered to the audience. As speakers vary, the information may vary but should have a similar essence because the foundational text is the same.

The Message

The message is the collective set of ideas that the speaker (the source) wants to deliver and/or illustrate to the audience. The message can be informative where the speaker informs the audience about a specific set of information. Or, the message may be persuasive in nature if the speaker wants to persuade the audience about conducting themselves in a specific manner, accepting God's commandments, or any number of things.

The Audience

The audience is the person or persons who are to receive the message. In the spiritual arena, there are many instances where an audience is present. It may be a traditional worship service, bible study, a conference, or a meeting. In any case, those who are there to receive the message from the audience, regardless of the number of individuals.

Dr. Cassundra White-Elliott

Where is Your Joppa?

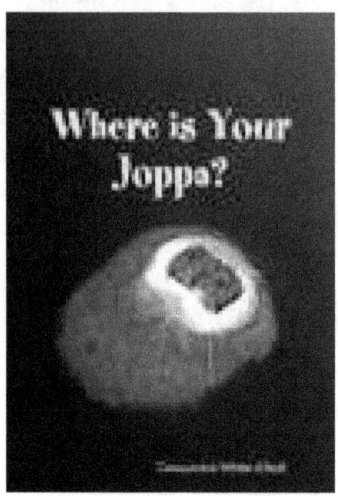

Introduction

Where is Your Joppa? was written for the express purpose of illustrating God's call for obedience in the lives of believers with respect to the individual call that He has on each of our lives. As you read throughout the various chapters, notice that the emphasis is placed on our persistent disobedience in answering God's call in a specific area of our lives. We have become a people who are similar to the Israelites when they found themselves in the middle of the wilderness, following their exodus from Egypt. Before God, they murmured and complained about their current life conditions and failed to be obedient to God's statutes delivered through His servant Moses. Their persistent disobedience caused them to lose the opportunity to see and enter the Promised Land. I ask you, "What has your disobedience cost you?" "Was your disobedience worth what it cost you?" "Do you think about the souls you could have ushered into the kingdom of God?" These are some of the questions that I pray will be answered through your reading of the book.

The first chapter following this introduction provides a detailed interpretation and analysis of the Book of Jonah, which serves as the foundational text for this book. Jonah, a prophet of God, commits an act of disobedience out of a spirit of pride and superiority. We, like Jonah, may also be afflicted with a spirit that prevents us from being obedient to God's call. Some of us are afflicted with pride, bitterness, unforgiveness, and rebellion, to name a few. These spirits are direct impediments to our obedience. However, others may not be afflicted with a spirit at all. We may be operating out of ignorance, not knowing that what we *are* doing is preventing us from what we *should* be doing.

Following the exegesis, the next three chapters (2-4) will provide examples of people today who walk in a spirit of disobedience. Using the theme "Joppa," I will pinpoint various situations that have occurred in the lives of several individuals that served as impediments to answering God-given mandates. What you may find surprising is that particular situations, relationships, or tasks that we may deem as honorable may indeed be impediments *if* we have allowed them to become a means of escape from what God has called us to do. So the situations themselves are not negative, but when we allow them to supersede God's call, our actions become negative. Reading these scenarios will prepare you for chapter five.

Chapter 5 discusses the necessity to perform a self evaluation. In order to see whether or not our lives indeed need to be turned around, we must be honest with ourselves about whether or not we have run from the call of God and situated ourselves in a safe haven, our very own "Joppa." When we honestly examine ourselves and allow the Holy Spirit to show us what lies deep within the recesses of our hearts, we provide ourselves with an opportunity to get our lives in order. Whether or not we actually make a change is something all together different.

After doing an honest assessment of our spiritual walk with God and unveiling any hidden "Joppas," we have to determine the right time to walk in obedience. Everyone has his/her own season for doing what God has mandated. Some of our seasons are right now, and some of our seasons are in a time to come. Knowing the right time to move is just as important as answering God's call. Therefore, Chapter 6 will discuss God's timing for us to move and for us to be still.

Finally, during the writing of this book, the Holy Spirit led me to appeal to the unbeliever. Chapter 7 is directed to the unbeliever, providing an opportunity for salvation.

As you read through the various chapters of the book, I pray that you will be receptive to the written words on the pages that were written under the direction of the Holy Spirit, as well as the words the Holy Spirit will undoubtedly speak directly to you about your own situation. Finally, do not hesitate to share this book with those whom the Holy Spirit leads you to.

I pray that the spirit of fear will not entrap you.

I pray that you will yield yourself as a willing vessel to our Heavenly Father.

I pray that you will answer the call that God has on your life.

Remember, I Samuel 15:22b states, "To obey is better than sacrifice."

Mayhem in the Hamptons

Romero and Yolanda optimistically plan for the day that is going to change their lives from being single persons to a couple who is united in holy matrimony. They, along with their parents, close friends and family, fly over to the infamous Hamptons, where only the rich and famous vacation, to have their dream wedding at the five-star Hampton Suites located on a peninsula in the Hamptons. Little do they know that their perfect day will turn out to be less than perfect when their wedding planner Mariesha Coleman suddenly goes missing!

A time when the newlyweds' lives should be filled with joy and the creation of wonderful memories, they are stricken with grief as they desperately try to find clues to help solve Mariesha's disappearance.

Mayhem in the Hamptons is a tale that shares how the horrors of a woman's past can come back to haunt her in more than one way and the impact it can have on anyone who gets in the way.

Preacher's Daughter

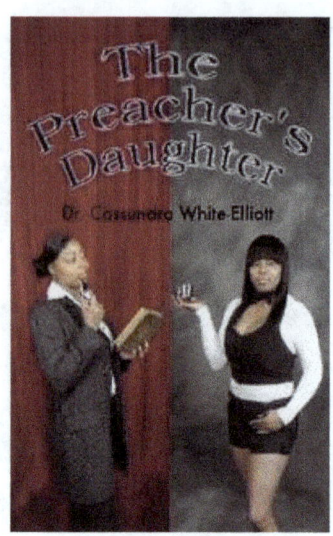

Tinisha, the daughter of a preacher, is a twenty-six year old God-fearing young woman endeavoring to complete law school so that she can make her mark in the courtroom.

Working in one of the late-night clubs in Hollywood to earn money to pay her own way through school, Tinisha soon learns that life doesn't always go as planned. Finding her strength in her faith, Tinisha constantly finds herself praying as she watches God move miraculously in her life.

Preacher's Son

Romero Turner is a private investigator with a promising future. As he continues to build his career, he is excited about the cases he undertakes. However, his father Pastor Theodore Turner has other plans for his son's life. In the midst of trying to save his client's husband from Sylvestor Domingo, a ruthless crime lord, Romero must try to salvage his relationship with his father. He must decide if ministry or life as a detective is in his future.

Lord, Teach Me to be a Blessing!

Lord, Teach Me to be a Blessing! will change a person's mentality from being centered around "me, myself, and I" to focusing on "others."

The world system teaches us that it is acceptable to place ourselves above others in an attempt to get ahead and even to survive. Herbert Spencer coined the phrase *'survival of the fittest'* after reading Charles Darwin's theory of evolution. This concept of surpassing and outdoing others is the world's philosophy.

However, the word of God does not subscribe to or promote this self-centered ideology, and therefore, neither should believers. We must hold fast to the truths outlined in Holy Scripture: "*Love thy neighbor as you love thyself*" (James 2:8) and "*It is more blessed to give than to receive*" (Acts 20:35).

While holding God's truths to be self evident, we must demonstrate them to others, thereby showing them the way of the Lord of how to be a blessing to someone *rather* than looking to receive a blessing.

This is the very purpose of this book: to change the mentality of the world from being *self* centered to *other* centered.

www.ingramcontent.com/pod-product-compliance
Lightning Source LLC
LaVergne TN
LVHW021714080426
835510LV00010B/988